Treasury of
Love Quotations
from
Many Lands

൙   ൙

Treasury of
Love Quotations
from
Many Lands

From the Editors of
Hippocrene Books
Illustrated by Lizbeth Nauta

HIPPOCRENE BOOKS, INC.
New York

For information, address:
HIPPOCRENE BOOKS, Inc.
171 Madison Avenue
New York, NY 10016

Library of Congress Cataloging-in-Publication Data available.

ISBN 0-7818-0574-0

Printed in the United States of America.

Contents

Eastern Antiquity

Ptah-hotep (Ancient Egyptian: 2300 B.C.)

Love thy wife as is fitting. Fill her belly; clothe her back; ointment is the prescription for her body. Make her heart glad as long as thou livest, for she is a profitable field for her lord.

Papyrus Haras 500 (Ancient Egyptian: 1600-1085 B.C.)

How splendid a whole day made holy by loving.

Prasnopanisad (Ancient India: circa 8th century B.C.)

Day and night are truly the masters of the world. Day is the abode of the spirit, and night the realm of the senses. Those who join their bodies during the day spill not just their seed but their very life. Those who pursue their loveplay in the time of stars know the true meaning of chastity.

Kathopanisad (Ancient India: 8th century B.C.)

People of small vision pursue sensual pleasures and walk into the trap that death has set, for the wise do not seek the eternal among perishable things. But who is it that enjoys the sights, tastes, smells, sounds and touches of love—who feels it? Who is it that knows? This, truly, is the point.

Confucius   (Chinese: 6th century B.C.)

To love a thing means wanting it to live.

Lao-Tse   (Chinese: circa 565 B.C.)

*By accident of fortune a man may rule the world for a time, but by
virtue of love, he may rule the world forever.*

Mahabharata   (Hindu: 540 B.C.-3rd century A.D.)

*The wife is half the man, the best of friends, the root of the three ends
of life, and of all that will help him in the other world.*

King Solomon   (Ancient Israel: circa 1st century B.C.)

Many waters cannot quench love, neither can floods drown it.

Love is strong as death; jealousy is cruel as the grave.

Comfort me with apples; for I am sick of love.

*It is better to dwell in a corner of the housetop, than with a brawling
woman in a wide house.*

Whoso findeth a wife findeth a good thing.

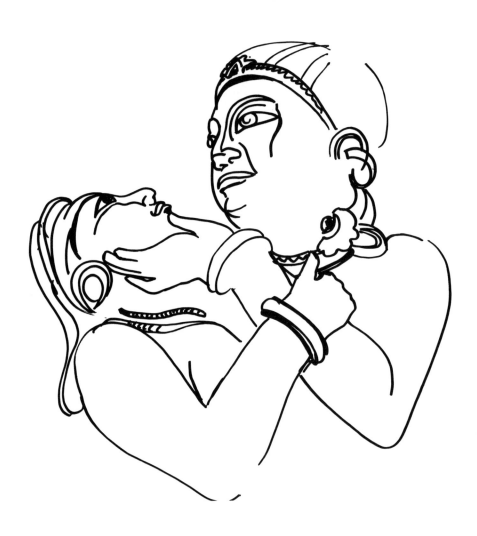

The Kama Sutra of Vatsyayana (Ancient India: 1st century A.D.)

When a man makes up to a woman, and she reproaches him with harsh words, she should be abandoned at once.

When a woman reproaches a man, but at the same time acts affectionately toward him, she should be made love to in every way.

A woman who hears a man playing on a reed pipe, which has been dressed with the juices of the bahupadika plant, becomes his slave.

The whole subject of embracing is such that men who ask questions about it, or who hear or talk about it, acquire a desire for enjoyment.

Men who generally obtain success with women are those well-versed in the science of love and who are celebrated for being very strong.

As variety is necessary in love, so love is to be produced by means of variety.

If variety is sought in all the arts and amusements, how much more should it be sought in the art of love.

There is a difference in the consciousness of pleasure, for a man thinks, 'This woman is united with me' and a woman thinks, 'I am united with this man.'

He who knows how to make himself beloved by women, as well as to increase their honor, becomes an object of their love.

Men and women, being of the same nature, feel the same kind of pleasure, and therefore a man should marry such a woman as will love him ever afterward.

Talmud   (Hebrew: 4th century A. D.)

The Lord gave more wit to women than to men.

More than a man wishes to marry, woman wishes to wed.

If a father marries off his daughter to a boor, it is as though he chained her and placed her before a lion.

Muhammed   (Islamic: 570-632)

He who is able to get married should; it keeps the eye cast down and keeps a man chaste. He who is unable should take to fasting, which will cool his passion.

Let no believing man hate his believing wife; if he is displeased with one trait of her character, let him be pleased with another that is within her.

The Poet Bassar   (Persian: 711-782)

I have exhausted my tears over the beloved, and have amazed my folk; yet I am no marvel—man before me has been befooled by passion, and carried away by love of girls.

Rabi'a Al-'Adawiyya   (Arabic: 712-801)

I loved you twice: because I am so passionate, because
you are so perfect.

Manyoshu Otomo Yakamoch   (Ancient Japan: 716-785)

Unknown love is as bitter a thing as the maiden-lily which grows in
the thickets of the summer moor.

A thing which fades with no outward signs—is the flower of the heart
of man in this world!

My love is like the grasses hidden in the deep mountain: though its
abundance increases, there is none that knows.

This longing for my love does not have seeds in time.

Kasa no Iratsume   (Japanese: 9th century)

To love someone who does not return that love is like offering prayers
back behind a starving god within a Buddhist temple.

Al-Mutanabbi   (Arabic: 915-965)

Real tears distinguish real lovers from fakes.

The Thousand and One Nights   (Arabic: 13th century)

Love was before the light began, when light is over, love shall be.

l-Yafi'i   (Arab Islamic: 1299-1367)

*They say: Thou art become mad with love for thy beloved. I reply:
The savor of life is for madmen.*

Wang Yang-ming   (Chinese: 1472-1529)

*[Love] is like a tree which shows the first signs of growth when the
shoot blossoms.*

ANCIENT GREECE AND ROME

Homer   (Ionian/Greek: early 13th century B.C.-mid 9th century B.C.)

Good for thee to have dalliance in a woman's arms.

Sappho   (Greek: 610 B.C.)

Love, like a mountain-wind upon an oak, falling upon me, shakes me leaf and bough.

Hipponax   (Greek: 6th century B.C.)

Two days are the best of a man's wedded life, the days when he marries and buries his wife.

Euripides   (Greek: circa 484-406 B.C.)

Love distills desire upon the eyes, love brings bewitching grace into the heart.

When cheated, wife or husband feels the same.

Socrates   (Greek: circa 470-399 B.C.)

As to marriage or celibacy, let man take which course he will, he is sure to repent.

Plato   (Greek: circa 427-347 B.C.)

*[Love is] the joy of the good, the wonder of the wise, the amazement of
the gods; desired by those who have no part in him, and precious to
those who have the better part in him.*

Menander   (Greek: 342-292 B.C.)

There is but one genuine love-potion—consideration.

Plautus   (Roman: 254-184 B.C.)

Where love is the seasoning, the dish will please everyone's taste.

He who craves food is no longer hungry once in love.

Show me a rational lover and I will give you his weight in gold.

*He who falls headlong into love suffers worse than if he had jumped
off a cliff.*

Love is like a missile, nothing is so swift in flight.

Love is a mixture of honey and bitterness.

*Blessed is he who loves, perish the man who cannot love, a double
death for the man who forbids love.*

The lover who sets out on the road of love with no money is in for more labors than Hercules.

Jupiter himself cannot separate two lovers against their own will.

A woman with the best perfume is one who has none.

Caecilius (Roman: circa 219-166 B.C.)

A man who does not believe that Love is the greatest god is either foolish or naive.

Terence (Roman: 185-159 B.C.)

The less my hope, the greater my love.

When lovers get angry their love revives.

I know the ways of women; when you want to, they don't; when you don't want to, they do.

There are many evils in love: suspicions, quarrels, wrongs and injustices, but war precedes peace.

Marcus Terentius Varro   (Roman: 116 -?27 B.C.)

Wise men love, others are mere lechers.

*Biting poverty and cruel Cupid are my foes. Hunger I can endure,
love I cannot.*

*Both king and poor man love; each carries the consuming
fire in his heart.*

Cicero   (Roman: 106-43 B.C.)

Nothing is too hard for him who loves.

Catullus   (Roman: 87-?54 B.C.)

*What a woman says to her lover should be written in the winds or on
the water.*

Virgil   (Roman: 70-19 B.C.)

It is a common complaint, we have all been in love at least once.

What may we not hope for when in love?

Horace   (Roman: 65-8 B.C.)

Love has two evils, war and then peace.

Cease hunting married game: trouble and grief more often come to you than real enjoyment.

Propertius   (Roman: circa 50-15 B.C.)

Venus is spoilt by serving her in darkness; surely you know, sight is the path of love.

I speak from experience, no one is faithful in love.

Medicine cures all human sufferings, but the sickness of love refuses a physician.

Either you conquer or you are conquered by the wheel of love.

No life is harder than that of a lover.

One is blind once stricken with love's madness.

Love may be delayed but not destroyed.

Cupid is naked and does not like artifices contrived by beauty.

A woman will do anything when she loves and hates.

He who will be my enemy, let him love women.

When my girl is sober, she pleases me a little; when she is drunk, she delights me.

Women's passions are more favorable toward an absent lover; long possession often lessens the desire of a lover.

Ovid   **(Roman: 43 B.C. -18 A.D.)**

If one wishes to escape idleness, let him fall in love.

Each lover is a soldier and Cupid has his own camp.

He who often says "I love not" is in love.

Modesty and love are not mutual concepts.

Nothing is more tender, or violent, than love.

Happy is he whom love's strife has downed.

Love is a thing replete with cares and fears.

Love often enters in the name of friendship.

The words of love do not respond to medicine and the healing art is of no avail to those in love.

Love fed fat soon turns to boredom.

Love is the naked child: do you think he has pockets for money?

Even chaste girls enjoy being praised for their beauty; virgins often worry about their looks.

To free himself from love, a man need only concentrate on his own problems.

A stolen love is pleasant to a man; it is also pleasant for a woman. The man dissembles badly, but the woman deceives much better.

Seneca   (Roman: circa 4 B.C.-65 A.D.)

It is easier to end love than to moderate it.

True love despises and will not tolerate delay.

One who is your friend always loves you, one who loves you is not always your friend.

Nothing grows again more easily than love.

Plutarch   (Greek: circa 46-120 A.D.)

When candles are out, all women are fair.

Tacitus   (Roman: circa 55-117 A.D.)

It is difficult to be moderate in love when you do not think it will last a long time.

Juvenal (Roman: circa 60-140 A.D.)

Many a fair nymph has in a cave been spread, and much good love without a feather bed.

Nothing is more savage than a woman motivated by shame.

St. Augustine (North African: 354-430 A.D.)

Inasmuch as love grows in you, so in you beauty grows. For love is the beauty of the soul.

He that is not jealous is not in love.

Boethius (Roman: 524 A.D.)

Who would give a law to lovers? Love is unto itself a higher law.

MEDIEVAL

Moses Ibn Ezra (Spanish: ?1055-1138)

Love blinds the eyes to faults, and hatred blinds them to virtues.

Peter Abélard (French: 1079-1142)

Love is a sickness that none can conceal; a look, a word, or even silence can reveal it.

Bernart de Ventadorn (Provençal: circa 1140-1180)

For God's sake, Love! I'm hardly fit to fight world conquerors such as you.

Rumi (Persian: 1207-1273)

Intellect in its effort to explain love got stuck in the mud like an ass. Love alone could explain love and loving.

A lover's life lies in death. You shall not find a heart without losing the heart.

Love possesses seven hundred wings, and each one extends from the highest heaven to the lowest earth.

Emperor Fushimi   (Japanese: 1265-1317)

In the midst of love I see one thing in everything within my gaze; not a tree, not a blade of grass, but a vision of you.

Dante Alighieri   (Italian: 1265-1321)

Love and the gentle heart are but a single thing.

Love, unkindled by virtue, always kindles another love, providing its flame shines forth.

Love insists that love should be mutual.

Hafiz   (Persian: 14th century)

Words have no language which can utter the secrets of love; and beyond the limits of expression is the expounding of desire.

He who has loved relates an endless tale. Here the most eloquent of tongue must fail.

Francisco Petrarca (PETRARCH)   (Italian: 1304-1374)

Love drives one not by choice but by fate.

To say how much you love is to love too little.

Giovanni Boccaccio   (**Italian: 1313-1375**)

Love, should I escape your snares, I doubt that I can be trapped by any other means.

Nijo Tameshige   (**Japanese: 1325-1385**)

If our love too is to follow the pattern of this world of lies, then what am I to do to make my own promise last?

Geoffrey Chaucer   (**English: circa 1343-1400**)

She loved right from first sight.

Wives, a random choice, untried that take, they dream in courtship, but in wedlock wake.

If there were no authority on earth except experience, mine, for what it's worth, and that's enough for me, all goes to show that marriage is a misery and a woe.

There's no creature in this world alive that without love has being or can thrive.

Thomas à Kempis   (**German: 1380-1471**)

Love is a great thing, a great good in every wise; it alone maketh light every heavy thing and beareth evenly every uneven thing.

Antoine de la Sale   (French: 1385-1460)

Love is selfishness for two.

Ausiàs March   (Catalan: ?1397-1459)

I've nausea now for all food else—excepting what's bought with love. That currency I'll pay.

I struggle against loving; wish to believe what thought assures me of, only cannot, cannot—no strength remaining after the long infirmity of love.

Marqués de Santillana   (Spanish: 1398-1458)

Love and you will be loved, and you will be able to do all that you could not do unloved.

How many people I've seen elevated by love, and how many more diminished by fear!

Sir Thomas Malory   (**English: circa 1408-1471**)

The heart must be free; it cannot be ordained whom we shall love.

. . . so fareth love nowadays, soon hot soon cold: this is no stability.

Today, we know, love is commonly as the summer or winter: brief and lewd, or cold and brittle—men cannot love seven nights but they must have their desires. In King Arthur's time this was not so: lovers remained true and fresh for seven years and more, and it was in honor of their ladies that knights bore arms and won glory.

Nezahualcoyotl   (**Aztec: 1418-1472**)

If you give your heart to each and every thing, you lead it nowhere; you destroy your heart.

Diego de San Pedro   (**Spanish: ?1437-?1498**)

The soul is measured by how much it suffers; life by how much it endures; the heart by how much it grieves; and the senses by how much they feel.

Jorge Manrique   (**Spanish: ?1440-?1479**)

Love is a power so powerful that it overpowers reason.

Louis XII   (French: 1462-1515)

Love is the young man's king and the old man's tyrant.

Renaissance

Juan del Encina   (Spanish: ?1468-1529)

A love without sorrow pleasure should not claim, for it is condemned by its feeble flame.

Nicolò Machiavelli   (Italian: 1469-1527)

It is far safer to be feared than loved.

Baldassare Castiglione   (Italian: 1478-1529)

One who loves much often talks little.

Martin Luther   (German: 1483-1546)

Who loves not wine, women or song, remains a fool his whole life long.

The procreation of mankind is a great marvel and mystery. Had God consulted me in the matter, I should have advised him to continue the generation by fashioning them out of clay, in the way Adam was fashioned.

Marguerite de Navarre   (French: 1492-1549)

I have heard much of these languishing lovers, but I never yet saw one of them die for love.

François Rabelais   (French: ?1494-1553)

I have seen it happen, often, to men who could not friggle when they wanted, because they hadn't wanted when they could.

Verily, I can do no more without a woman than a blind man without his staff; my gimlet must drill or I could not live.

Marry? . . . Better drain a cup of shame than play the wedding-game.

Giovanni Battista Giraldi   (Italian: 1504-1573)

It is a sign of a noble heart when a young man burns with a flame of love.

Mihri Hatun   (Turkish: d. 1506)

At one glance I love you with a thousand hearts.

Santa Teresa de Jesús   (Spanish:1515-1582)

It is love alone that gives worth to all things.

Love is never lazy.

Motecuhzoma II　　　　　　　　　　　　　　　　　　(Aztec: d. 1520)

Beauty! You have come before lords, open to love on my feather mat.

Michel de Montaigne　　　　　　　　　　　　　　　(French: 1533-1592)

Love has compensations which friendship does not.

Marriage is a covenant which hath nothing free but the entrance.

I see no marriages fail sooner, or more troubled, than such as are concluded for beauty's sake, and huddled up for amorous desires.

Battista Guarini　　　　　　　　　　　　　　　　　(Italian: 1538-1612)

Kisses, when given in love, are the joining together of two loving souls.

He who has been smitten by the arrows of love is no longer afraid of any other wound.

Fernando de Rojas　　　　　　　　　　　　　　　　(Spanish: d. 1541)

[Love] is a hidden fire, a pleasant sore, a delicious poison, a sweet bitterness, a delectable pain, an agreeable torment, a sweet and throbbing wound, a gentle death.

San Juan de la Cruz　　　　　　　　　　　　　　　(Spanish: 1542-1591)

Where love does not exist, plant it and it will grow.

Torquato Tasso   (Italian: 1544-1595)

Any time that is not spent on love is wasted.

I would advise a sane man to receive love.

How sweet is the rapturous state of soft passions in a heart full of love.

Miguel de Cervantes   (Spanish: 1547-1616)

One could ne'er call ill-fated a love that is requited.

Love in young men, for the most part, is not love at all but simply sexual desire and its accomplishment is its end.

The eyes are the silent tongues of love.

Giordano Bruno   (Italian: 1548-1600)

We are surrounded by eternity and by the uniting of love. There is but one center from which all species issue, as rays from a sun, and to which all species return.

Sir Philip Sidney   (English: 1554-1586)

They love indeed who quake to say they love.

John Lyly (English: ?1554-1606)

Men in matters of love have as many ways to deceive as they have words to utter.

To love women and never enjoy them, is as much to love wine and never taste it.

Women that delight in courting are wont to yield.

George Chapman (English: 1559-1634)

Love is Nature's second sun.

Francis Bacon (English: 1561-1626)

Wives are young men's mistresses, companions for middle age, and old men's nurses.

Nuptial love maketh mankind; friendly love perfecteth it; but wanton love corrupteth it and embaseth it.

Lope de Vega (Spanish: 1562-1635)

Harmony is pure love, for love is a concerto.

Beware, love is deaf as a stone, and will listen not to words the day he sits on the throne.

Christopher Marlowe (**English: 1564-1593**)

Who ever loved, that loved not at first sight?

William Shakespeare (**English: 1564-1616**)

There lives within the very flame of love
A kind of wick or snuff that will abate it.

What is love? 'Tis not hereafter; present mirth hath present laughter;
What's to come is still unsure.

The course of true love never did run smooth.

If thou remember'st not the slightest folly that ever love did make thee
run into, thou hast not loved.

Love is a spirit all compact of fire, not gross to sink, but light,
and will aspire.

Love is too young to know what conscience is; yet who knows not con-
science is born of love?

Men have died from time to time and worms have eaten them,
but not for love.

Young men's love then lies not truly in their hearts, but in their eye.

Many a good hanging prevents a bad marriage.

By heaven, I do love: and it hath taught me to rhyme and
be melancholy.

Thomas Middleton (English: 1570-1627)

In the election of a wife, as in a project of war, to err but once is to be undone forever.

John Donne (English: 1572-1631)

Love built on beauty, soon as beauty, dies.

Love, all alike, no season knows, nor clime, nor hours, age, months, which are the rags of time.

I am two fools, I know for loving, and for saying so in whining poetry.

Robert Burton (English: 1577-1640)

A true saying it is, desire hath no rest.

Phineas Fletcher (English: 1582-1650)

Love is like linen often changed, the sweeter.

Tirso de Molina (Spanish: 1584-1648)

Love is like a king that, with just law, rends alike silk and sackcloth.

Nahabed Kouchag   (Armenian: d. 1592)

Whoever loves and finds no cure, let him dig his grave and enter alive.

René Descartes   (French: 1596-1650)

Love is much better than hatred; there is never too much.

Baroque Period:
The 17th and 18th Centuries

Tschu-Li (Chinese: 1606-1645)

The spirit that endows all things with life is love.

Madeleine de Scudéry (French: 1607-1701)

Love is a passion which surrenders to nothing, but to the contrary, everything surrenders to love.

John Milton (English: 1608-1674)

What seemed fair in all the world seemed now mean . . . and in her looks, which from that time infused sweetness into my heart, unfelt before, and into all things from her air, inspired the spirit of love and amorous delight.

François de La Rochefoucauld (French: 1613-1680)

There is only one kind of love, but there are a thousand different copies.

The pleasure of love is in the loving. We are happier in the passion we feel than in that which we excite.

True love is like ghosts, which everybody talks about and few have seen.

Love, like fire, can only exist in eternal movement, and love ceases to live as soon as it ceases hoping and fearing.

There are few people who are not ashamed of their love affairs when the infatuation is over.

You keep your first love longer when you don't take a second one.

Charles Saint-Evremond   (French: 1613-1703)

Love does not hurt ladies' reputations, unless their lovers lack merit.

Abraham Cowley   (English: 1618-1667)

Never, my dear, was honor yet undone, by love, but indiscretion.

Ninon de Lenclos   (French: 1620-1705)

Love is a traitor who scratches us even when we want only to play with him.

Love never dies of want, but often of indigestion.

Jean de La Fontaine (French: 1621-1695)

Love, love, when you hold us in your grasp we can say farewell to caution.

Jean-Baptiste Poquelin, Molière (French: 1622-1673)

The whole pleasure of love is in its variety.

We are easily duped by those whom we love.

There is something inexpressibly charming in falling in love and, surely, the whole pleasure lies in the fact that love isn't lasting.

Love is often a consequence of marriage.

Thomas Corneille (French: 1625-1709)

True love is like a sigh from the heart; it teaches in a moment every-thing one ought to say.

John Dryden (English: 1631-1700)

Pains of love be sweeter far than all other pleasures are.

Heaven be thanked, we live in such an age when no man dies for love, but on the stage.

Samuel Pepys   (English: 1633-1703)

Strange to say what delight we married people have to see poor fools decoyed into our condition.

Jean Racine   (French: 1639-1699)

Love eagerly believes everything it wishes.

The heart that can no longer love passionately must with fury hate.

Jean de La Bruyère   (French: 1645-1696)

Love that springs suddenly into being takes the longest to cure.

Love alone begets love. The strongest of friendships could only become a weak love.

Gottfried Wilhelm von Leibniz   (German: 1646-1716)

To love is to place our happiness in the happiness of another.

Juana Ines de la Cruz   (Mexican: 1651-1695)

As love is union, it knows no extremes of distance.

Abu Firas (Arabic: 1654-1734)

We can melt steel, but are easily melted by beautiful eyes.

Jean François Régnard (French: 1655-1709)

When love talks, reason must be silent.

Love is fond of spontaneous action.

William Congreve (English: 1670-1729)

Words are the weak support of cold indifference; love has no language to be heard.

If this be not love, it is madness, and then it is pardonable.

Courtship to marriage, as a very witty prologue to a very dull play.

Tho' marriage makes man and wife one flesh, it leaves 'em still two fools.

Colley Cibber (English: 1671-1757)

Oh! how many torments lie in the small circle of a wedding-ring!

Our hours in love have wings; in absence, crutches.

John Gay (**English: 1685-1732**)

The comfortable estate of widowhood is the only hope that keeps up a wife's spirits.

Alexander Pope (**English: 1688-1744**)

Love, free as air at sight of human ties, spreads his light wings, and in a moment flies.

They dream in courtship, but in wedlock wake.

Samuel Richardson (**English: 1689-1761**)

Love, at first sight, supposes such susceptibility of passion, as, however it may pass in a man, very little becomes the delicacy of the female character.

Kelemen Mikes (**Hungarian: 1690-1761**)

Never compliment a woman in front of other women, because none of them will like it.

François-Marie Arouet, VOLTAIRE　　　　　　　　(French: 1694-1778)

Love is the cloth which imagination embroiders.

Pleasure has its time; so, too, has wisdom. Make love in thy youth, and in old age attend to thy salvation.

from *Parang Sabil of Abdullah and Putli Izra*　　　(Philippino: 18th century)

Though on earth we are unwed, in heaven we shall be united.

Benjamin Franklin　　　　　　　　　　　　　　(American: 1706-1790)

Keep your eyes wide open before marriage, half shut afterwards.

In your amours you should prefer old women to young ones. They are so grateful.

You can't pluck roses without fear of thorns. Nor enjoy a fair wife without fear of horns.

Samuel Johnson　　　　　　　　　　　　　　　(English: 1709-1784)

Love is the wisdom of the fool and the folly of the wise.

A man is in general better pleased when he has a good dinner upon the table than when his wife talks Greek.

Marriage has many pains, but celibacy has no pleasures.

Jean-Jacques Rousseau   (French: 1712-1778)

To love and be loved will be the greatest event in our lives.

Debauchery and love cannot live together.

Luc de Clapiers Vauvernargues   (French: 1715-1747)

Love is stronger than self-love, since we can love a woman
who scorns us.

Oliver Goldsmith   (Irish: 1728-1747)

Friendship is disinterested commerce between equals; love, an object
intercourse between tyrants and slaves.

Gottfried Ephraim Lessing   (German: 1729-1781)

For without love, or wine, now own! What would thou be,
O man?—A stone.

Equality is always the strongest tie of love.

P.A.C. de Beaumarchais   (French: 1732-1799)

Where love is concerned, too much is not even enough!

Desire places us at the feet of women, but in time, the pleasure
subdues them.

Nicholas Chamfort (French: 1741-1794)

In love, everything is true, everything is false; it is the one subject on which one cannot express an absurdity.

When they approach thirty years of age, women begin to save their love letters.

Love is like an epidemic; the more one is afraid, the more vulnerable one is.

György Bessenyei (Hungarian: 1747-1811)

It is true, that everywhere it is the men who command and lead their household, but it is the women who develop in them that secret instinct, which makes them seek peace and happiness.

Johann Wolfgang von Goethe (German: 1749-1832)

One virtue stands out above all others: the constant striving upwards, wrestling with oneself, the unquenchable desire for greater purity, wisdom, goodness, and love.

A life without love, without the presence of the beloved, is nothing but a mere magic-lantern show. We draw out slide after slide, swiftly tiring of each, and pushing it back to make haste for the next.

Vamekesvaratantram (Indian: before 1750)

If you must learn about sexual love, learn from an expert that it is founded in compassion.

Richard Brinsley Sheridan (Irish: 1751-1816)

'Tis safest in matrimony to begin with a little aversion.

Robert Burns (Scottish: 1759-1796)

O my luve is like a red, red rose that's newly sprung in June. O my luve is like the melodie that's sweetly play'd in tune.

Friedrich Schiller (German: 1759-1805)

No emperor has power to prescribe laws for the heart.

Ferenc Kazinczy (Hungarian: 1759-1831)

Isn't it better to love one, rather than to embrace many?

Madame de Staël   (French: 1766-1817)

Love is above the laws, above the opinion of men; it is the truth, the flame, the pure element, the primary idea of the moral world.

Love is the very history of a woman's life, it is merely an episode in a man's.

Henri de Rebecque, Benjamin Constant   (French: 1767-1830)

Love is the most selfish of all emotions, thus the least generous when hurt.

James Hogg   (Scottish: 1770-1835)

O Love, love, love! Love is like a dizziness; It winna let a poor body gang about his biziness!

Sir Walter Scott   (Scottish: 1771-1832)

Love rules the court, the camp, the grove, and men below, and saints above; for love is heaven and heaven is love.

Samuel Taylor Coleridge (English: 1772-1824)

*In many ways doth the full heart reveal the presence of love
it would conceal.*

Sympathy constitutes friendship; but in love there is a sort of antipathy, or opposing passion. Each strives to be the other, and both together make up one whole.

A man's desire is for the woman; but the woman's desire is rarely other than for the desire of the man.

The most happy marriage I can picture or imagine to myself would be the union of a deaf man to a blind woman.

Sándor Kisfaludy (Hungarian: 1772-1844)

*Love is the earth, water, fire, sky,— And still you don't recognize it?
Just peer into your heart, it'll teach you.*

The brain causes a thousand problems;—One can avoid these; The heart, since it's rapacious, is a lot harder to escape.

Jane Austen (English: 1775-1817)

A lady's imagination is very rapid; it jumps from admiration to love, from love to matrimony, in a moment.

Is not general incivility the very essence of love?

THE 19TH CENTURY

Ugo Foscolo **(Italian: 1778-1827)**

The happiness of being in love sweetens whatever pain exists.

The joy of love promotes and sustains it.

Charles Caleb Colton **(English: 1780-1832)**

Marriage is a feast where the grace is sometimes better than the dinner.

Madame Swetchine **(French: 1782-1857)**

To love deeply in one direction makes us more loving in all others.

Marie-Henri Beyle, STENDHAL **(French: 1783-1842)**

Love is a pleasure that torments as it pleases.

Love is a trifling thing, and yet it is the only weapon that can wound a stout heart.

Love is a haughty despot; he will have all or nothing.

True love makes the thought of death frequent, easy, without terrors; it merely becomes the standard of comparison, the price one would pay for many things.

The greatest happiness that love can give is the first handclasp of the woman you love.

The most beautiful part of life is concealed from a man who has not loved with passion.

Thomas Love Peacock (English: 1785-1866)

Marriage may often be a stormy lake, but celibacy is almost always a muddy horsepond.

Elizabeth Patterson Bonaparte (American: 1785-1879)

Even quarrels with one's husband are preferable to the ennui of a solitary existence.

Justinus Kerner (German: 1786-1862)

Love is deepest aching.

Countess of Blessington (English: 1789-1849)

Love matches are formed by people who pay for a month of honey with a life of vinegar.

Theodor Körner   (German: 1791-1813)

Love hath no measurement in time; it buds and blooms and ripens in one glowing hour.

József Katona   (Hungarian: ?1791-1830)

A free glance, a free heart, freely spoken words, hand in hand and eye to eye,—this is how love is by us: whoever kneels here, is either praying, or acting.

To laugh or to shed a tear; it makes no difference for women.

Oh, there is nothing more despicable than to take advantage of a woman's weakness!

Many men—and I know this about myself—will not love a woman who promises to be an easy victory; but if the conquest is difficult, then out of sheer pride, they will fall in love with her.

Percy Bysshe Shelley   (English: 1792-1822)

All love is sweet, given or returned.

Familiar acts are beautiful through love.

John Clare   **(English: 1793-1864)**

Say, what is love? A blooming name, a rose-leaf on the page of fame, that blows, then fades, to cheat no more, and is what nothing was before?

Aleksander Fredro   **(Polish: 1793-1876)**

No man has yet died of love.

An old lover is like an old stove: much smoke, little steam.

John Keats   **(English: 1795-1821)**

Love in a hut, with water and a crust, is —Love forgive us!—cinders, ashes, dust; Love in a palace is perhaps at last more grievous torment than a hermit's fast.

Love is my religion—I could die for it.

Count Giacomo Leopardi   **(Italian: 1798-1837)**

Love is the ultimate deception of our life.

D'Azeglio   (Italian: 1798-1866)

True love is a grand treasure; it is the greatest treasure that exists.

Jules Michelet   (French: 1798-1874)

Woman is a miracle of divine contradictions.

Honoré de Balzac   (French: 1799-1850)

Love is the only passion that cares not about the past or the future.

Those in love either doubt nothing or doubt everything.

To love without hope is still happiness.

Passion is in all humanity; without it, religion, history, literature, and art would be rendered useless.

Love which economizes is never true love.

Man can start with aversion and end with love, but if he begins with love and comes around to aversion he will never get back to love.

The man who enters his wife's dressing room is either a philosopher or a fool.

The bonds of wedlock are so heavy it takes two to carry them— sometimes three.

A man cannot marry before he has studied anatomy and has dissected at least one woman.

Alexandre Dumas fils (French: 1802-1870)

Without respect love cannot go far or rise high; it is an angel with only one wing.

Love is the war of the sexes. Both sides know their objective and all is fair to attain it.

Tommaseo (Italian: 1802-1874)

There are only two things certain about love: distress and ignorance.

Victor Hugo (French: 1802-1885)

The supreme happiness of life is the conviction that we are loved.

The first symptom of love in a young man is shyness; the first symptom in a young woman is boldness.

Love is an ocean and a woman is the shore.

A woman with one lover is an angel, a woman with two lovers is a monster, a woman with three lovers is a woman.

Douglas Jerrold (English: 1803-1857)

Love's like the measles—all the worse when it comes late in life.

E.G. Bulwer-Lytton (**English: 1803-1873**)

Love is the business of the idle, but the idleness of the busy.

Ralph Waldo Emerson (**American: 1803-1897**)

Marriage is the perfection which love aimed at, ignorant of what it sought.

Guerrazzi (**Italian: 1804-1873**)

Love grows and wanes in the heart of man.

George Sand (**French: 1804-1876**)

There is only one happiness in life, to love and be loved.

No human creature can give orders to love.

Benjamin Disraeli (**English: 1804-1881**)

The magic of first love is our ignorance that it can ever end.

I have always thought that every woman should marry, and no man.

Elizabeth Barrett Browning (English: 1806-1861)

How do I love thee? Let me count the ways. I love thee to the depth and breadth and height my soul can reach . . .

Julian Korsak (Polish: 1807-1855)

Feminine beauty attracts us more than all the wisdom of the world.

Alphonse Karr (French: 1808-1890)

Love is like a bird that sings in the hearts of women.

Louis Charles Alfred de Musset (French: 1810-1857)

Life is a long sleep and love is its dream.

The only true language in the world is a kiss.

To love, that's the point—what matters whom? What does the bottle matter provided we can be drunk?

William Makepeace Thackeray (English: 1811-1863)

To love and win is the best thing; to love and lose, the next best.

Zygmunt Krasinski (Polish: 1812-1859)

Unhappiness, like love, binds people together.

Søren Aabye Kierkegaard (Danish: 1813-1855)

When one has once fully entered the realm of love, the world—no matter how imperfect—becomes rich and beautiful, for it consists solely of opportunities for love.

Mikhail Lermontov (Russian: 1814-1841)

Love, like fire, dies out without fuel. Perhaps jealousy will succeed where my pleas have failed.

Russian young ladies for the most part go on only for Platonic love with no intention of matrimony, and Platonic love is most disturbing...

What would a woman not do to hurt her rival!

Anthony Trollope (English: 1815-1882)

Don't let love interfere with your appetite. It never does with mine.

Henry David Thoreau　　　　　　　　　　　　　　　　(American: 1817-1862)

Between whom there is hearty truth there is love . . .

There is no remedy for love but to love more.

Love is the burden of all nature's odes; the song of the birds is an epithalamium, a hymneal. The marriage of the flowers spots the meadows and fringes the hedges with pearls and diamonds.

Emily Brontë　　　　　　　　　　　　　　　　　　　(English: 1818-1848)

Love is like the wild rose-briar; friendship like the holly tree. The holly is dark when the rose-briar blooms, but which will bloom more constantly?

Ivan Turgenev　　　　　　　　　　　　　　　　　　(Russian: 1818-1883)

Love is stronger than death and more powerful than all fear of dying. Life lives only through love.

John Ruskin　　　　　　　　　　　　　　　　　　　(English:1819-1900)

When love and skill work together, expect a masterpiece.

Bozena Nemcova (Czech: 1820-1862)

Even if man would be fully satisfied with everything else, he will always crave more love.

Love is a disease, but it does not want to be healed.

Sepritun Yantush (Chuvash: 1821-1861)

The bride wails tearfully and repeats these words: "Oh father, oh mother! you haven't loved me, you have deserted me—you are giving me away."

Charles Baudelaire (French: 1821-1867)

After a debauch, one feels oneself to be more solitary, more abandoned.

Fyodor Dostoyevsky (Russian: 1821-1881)

In order to love simply, it is necessary to know how to show love.

With love one can live even without happiness.

To love someone means to see him as God intended him.

Henri Fréderic Amiel   (Swiss: 1821-1881)

Knowledge, love, power—there is the complete life.

Thomas Fuller   (English: 1822-1898)

Though love is blind, yet 'tis not for want of eyes.

Keep the eyes wide open before marriage; and half-shut afterward.

Sándor Petofi   (Hungarian: 1823-1849)

*Freedom and love, these two things I need. For love I sacrifice my life,
for freedom I sacrifice my love.*

Love makes up for everything, but nothing makes up for love.

Alexander Druzhinin   (Russian: 1824-1864)

In love there is a lot of gratitude for former pleasures.

*A good wife is of that kind a luxury for the sake of which one may
give up much excess.*

*A woman not capable of involving her husband is like a miserly
mother who poorly feeds her children.*

Bayard Taylor   (American: 1825-1878)

The loving are the daring.

Mór Jókai   (Hungarian: 1825-1904)

Man's destiny is woman.

Jan Zachariasiewicz   (Polish: 1825-1906)

*Love is a dainty golden little box, in which you will find a carefully
prepared and concealed little bill.*

George Meredith   (English: 1828-1909)

Kissing don't last: cookery do!

Leo Tolstoy   (Russian: 1828-1910)

*If so many men, so many minds, certainly so many hearts, so many
kinds of love.*

*To say that you can love one person all your life is like saying that one
candle will continue to burn as long as you live.*

Emily Dickinson   (American: 1830-1886)

Unable are the loved to die, for Love is immortality.

Nievo   (Italian: 1831-1861)

Love is a spontaneous grass, not a plant which is carefully cultivated in the garden.

Louisa May Alcott   (American: 1832-1888)

Love is a great beautifier.

Jan Neruda   (Czech: 1834-1891)

Do not ever believe a person who says that he does not care for love. Such a person is either very envious, or is a little, quite little and poor, love-beggar who is ashamed of his begging.

Samuel Butler   (English: 1835-1902)

God is Love, I dare say. But what a mischievous Devil Love is.

Mark Twain   (American: 1835-1910)

To get the full value of joy you must have someone to divide it with.

Love seems the swiftest, but it is the slowest of all growths. No man or woman really knows what perfect love is until they have been married a quarter of a century.

Familiarity breeds contempt—and children.

Gustavo Adolfo Bécquer   (Spanish: 1836-1870)

The soul that can speak with the eyes, can also kiss with a gaze.

Gabriele D'Annunzio   (Italian: 1836-1938)

He who is in love is often compelled to deceive.

Rosalía de Castro   (Galician: 1837-1885)

When I fell in love—and little thanks I had of it—I threw my life away, believing you my earth and heaven too.

Eugenio Maria de Hostos   (Puerto Rican: 1839-1903)

Nearly all human beings love, but nearly none know how to love.

Taras Stevchenko   (Ukrainian: 1840-1861)

The heart will find its doom in love. So, let it throb with pain till it is in the tomb!

Alphonese Daudet   (French: 1840-1897)

Ideal love is a delusion put forth by poets.

Émile Zola   (French: 1840-1902)

Love, like swallows, brings luck to a home.

Ambrose Bierce   (American: 1842-1914)

"Love,": A temporary insanity curable by marriage.

Friedrich Nietzche   (German: 1844-1900)

Love brings to light the noble and hidden qualities of a lover—his rare and exceptional traits: to that extent it conceals his usual character.

Love is more afraid of change than destruction.

There is always some madness in love. But there is also always some reason in madness.

When a man is in love he endures more than at other times; he submits to everything.

It is not a lack of love, but a lack of friendship that makes unhappy marriages.

Anatole France   (French: 1844-1924)

A woman in love neither fears hell nor envies paradise.

Edward Carpenter   (English: 1844-1929)

Real love is only possible in the freedom of society; and freedom is only possible when love is a reality.

Henryk Sienkiewicz   (Polish: 1846-1916)

Love is not blind: it just changes eyes into prisms and shows the world as rainbow-hued.

Giuseppe Giacosa   (Italian: 1847-1906)

Sad is the house where love does not live.

Boleslaw Prus (Polish: 1847-1912)

An old man with a young wife is like a bookbinder. He binds a book another man reads.

Ellen Key (Swedish: 1849-1926)

Love has been in perpetual strife with monogamy.

Aleksander Swietochowski (Polish: 1849-1938)

You will learn more wisdom from one wife than from a thousand mistresses.

Guy de Maupassant (French: 1850-1893)

The most beautiful women are made for lovers who lack imagination.

Robert Louis Stevenson (Scottish: 1850-1894)

Marriage is like life in this—that it is a field of battle, and not a bed of roses.

Mirza-Shafi Vazekh (Azerbaijani: d. 1852)

Let Satan have my soul—I'll have my bliss.

Paul Bourget (French: 1852-1935)

Love that survives jealousy is like a pretty face after smallpox; a bit pockmarked forever after.

The proof that experience teaches us nothing is that the end of one love does not prevent us from beginning another.

Jaroslav Vrchlicky (Czech: 1853-1912)

Love is a treasure not diminished by time; . . . it is the smile of the day and the miracle of the night.

Arthur Rimbaud (French: 1854-1891)

Love must be reinvented.

Oscar Wilde   (Irish: 1854-1900)

When one is in love one begins by deceiving one's self. And one ends by deceiving others. That is what the world calls a romance.

How marriage ruins a man. It's as demoralizing as cigarettes, and far more expensive.

Men marry because they are tired; women because they are curious. Both are disappointed.

Those who are faithless know the pleasures of love; it is those who are faithful who know love's tragedies.

She wore far too much rouge last night and not quite enough clothes. That is always a sign of despair in a woman.

Ultimately, the bond of all companionship, whether in marriage or friendship, is conversation.

Nowadays all married men live like bachelors, all bachelors live like married men.

The world has grown suspicious of anything that looks like a happily married life.

Twenty years of romance make a woman look like a ruin; but twenty years of marriage make her something like a public building.

Sigmund Freud   (Austrian: 1856-1939)

How bold one gets when one is sure of being loved!

Love cannot be much younger than the lust for murder.

George Bernard Shaw (Irish: 1856-1950)

When we want to read of the deeds that are done for love, whither do we turn? To the murder column.

There is no love sincerer than the love of food.

What God hath joined together no man shall ever put asunder: God will take care of that.

Shalom Aleichem (Russian: 1859-1916)

Love is sweet but it's tastier with a piece of bread.

A husband—even if he has sinned—is still a husband.

Go understand a girl: she looks forward to her wedding, and weeps when she walks to the marriage canopy.

Jules Laforgue (French: 1860-1887)

Love is a pure dew which drops from heaven into our heart.

Anton Chekhov (Russian: 1860-1904)

Women deprived of the company of men pine, men deprived of the company of women become stupid.

Luckily for men, women in love are always blinded by love and never know life.

The presence of a beloved woman . . . produces an effect similar to music and wine.

Gabriela Zapolska (Polish: 1860-1921)

As long as a woman is desired, she does not get old.

Karel Matej Capek-Chod (Czech: 1860-1927)

Love without a quarrel is like a peacock without feathers.

Bliss Carman (Canadian: 1861-1929)

Love manifests itself in our bodies as instinctive craving, in our souls as devotion, and in our minds as pride.

Henri François Joseph de Régnier (French: 1864-1936)

When in love one often speaks of love too much but does not prove it enough.

Miguel de Unamuno   (Spanish: 1864-1936)

Love! love always getting in the way of great deeds! How much time has humanity lost for love's blessed sake!

The 20th Century

Rabindranath Tagore (Indian: 1861-1941)

Love is an endless mystery, for it has nothing else to explain it.

Let the dead have the immortality of fame, but the living the immortality of love.

Love remains a secret even when spoken, for only a love truly knows that he is loved.

Love's gift cannot be given, it waits to be accepted.

In love all of life's contradictions dissolve and disappear. Only in love are unity and duality not in conflict.

Francis W.L. Adams (Australian: 1862-1893)

Of all Love's speeches, silence is the best.

George Santayana (Spanish: 1863-1952)

Love, whether sexual, parental, or fraternal, is essentially sacrificial, and prompts a man to give his life for his friends.

Miguel de Unamuno (Spanish: 1864-1936)

We shall not create geniuses through pedagogy until we have eliminated love.

Love is the child of illusion and the parent of disillusion.

Rudyard Kipling   (English: 1865-1936)

Take my word for it, the silliest woman can manage a clever man, but it takes a very clever woman to manage a fool.

William Butler Yeats   (Irish: 1865-1939)

Hearts are not had as a gift but hearts are earned.

A pity beyond all telling is in the heart of love.

Never give all the heart, for love will hardly seem worth thinking of to passionate women if it seems certain.

Paul Jean Toulet   (French: 1867-1920)

Love is like those second rate hotels where all the luxury is in the lobby.

A woman who loves her husband is merely paying her bills. A woman who loves her lover gives alms to the poor.

Paul Claudel   (French: b. 1868)

One who loves with passion cannot easily forgive.

Maxim Gorky (Russian: 1868-1936)

When one loves somebody, everything is clear—where to go, what to do—it all takes care of itself and one doesn't have to ask anybody about anything.

When a woman gets married it's like jumping into a hole in the ice in the middle of winter: you do it once, and you remember it the rest of your days.

Stephen B. Leacock (Canadian: 1869-1944)

One-sided love lasts best.

Mohandas K. Gandhi (Indian: 1869-1948)

Love is the strongest force the world possesses, and yet it is the humblest imaginable.

Whenever you are confronted with an opponent, conquer him with love.

André Gide (French: 1869-1951)

The greatest pleasure next to loving is to confess your love.

Too chaste an adolescence makes for a dissolute old age.

Henri Matisse (French: 1869-1954)

Wine comes in at the mouth; love comes in through the eye.

Christopher Brennan (Australian: 1870-1932)

Love set his fire in my hands; I clasped the flame onto my heart.

Marcel Proust (French: 1871-1922)

*Those whose suffering is due to love are, as we say of certain invalids,
their own physicians.*

Paul Valéry (French: 1871-1945)

Everything is magic in the relationship between a man and a woman.

Bertrand Russell (English: b. 1872)

*Love as a relation between men and women was ruined by the desire
to make sure of the legitimacy of children.*

*To fear love is to fear life, and those who fear life are already three
parts dead.*

Simazaki Toson (Japanese: 1872-1943)

Love is no fox, nor you a bunch of grapes. But unbeknown my heart stole out and plucked you in secret, when no one was about.

Max Beerbohm (English: 1872-1956)

Women who love the same man have a kind of bitter freemasonry.

Valery Lakolevich Briusov (Russian: 1873-1924)

How many people surrender themselves to love not knowing its laws.

Maryla Wolska (Polish: 1873-1930)

Nothing moves a man more than the tears of a woman he has begun to love, and nothing irritates him more than the tears of a woman whom he has stopped loving.

G.K. Chesterton (English: 1874-1936)

The way to love anything is to realize that it might be lost.

Nikolai Aleksandrovich Berdyayev   (Russian: 1874-1948)

The physical union of the sexes only intensifies man's sense of solitude.

Robert Frost   (American: 1874-1963)

Love is an irresistible desire to be irresistibly desired.

Winston Churchill   (English: 1874-1965)

My wife and I tried two to three times in the last forty years to have breakfast together, but it was so disagreeable that we had to stop.

W. Somerset Maugham   (English: 1874-1965)

The great tragedy in life is not that men perish, but that they cease to love.

It takes two to make a love affair and a man's meat is too often a woman's poison.

Women's hearts are like old china, none the worse for a break or two.

No woman is worth more than a fiver unless you're in love with her. Then she's worth all she costs you.

Rainer Maria Rilke (German: 1875-1926)

For one human being to love another: that is perhaps the most diffi-cult of all our tasks, the ultimate, the last test and proof, the work for which all other work is but preparation.

Love consists in this, that two solitudes protect and touch and greet each other.

Helen Rowland (American: 1875-1950)

A husband is what is left of a lover, after the nerve has been extracted.

Thomas Mann (German: 1875-1955)

He who loves the more is the inferior and must suffer.

It is love, not reason, that is stronger than death.

Aino Kallas (Finnish: 1878-1956)

Love is like the measles, only up to a certain age is it a childhood dis-ease and as such harmless; later it becomes deadly.

Carl Sandburg (**American: 1878-1967**)

There is a warning love sends and the cost of it is never written till long afterward.

Yong-woon Han (**Korean: 1879-1944**)

Love after all is a human affair, so I feared our separation since we first met.

A love song that cannot bear its own music hovers over the love's silence.

James Branch Cabell (**American: 1879-1958**)

People marry through a variety of other reasons and with varying results; but to marry for love is to invite inevitable tragedy.

E. M. Forster (**English: 1879-1970**)

Love is a great force in private life; it is indeed the greatest of all things; but love in public affairs does not work.

Maria Gustava Jotuni   (Finnish: 1880-1943)

If love takes even a sixty year old by surprise, imagine what it can do to a twenty year old.

H.L. Mencken   (American: 1880-1956)

The most disgusting cad in the world is the man who, on grounds of decorum and morality, avoids the game of love. He is one who puts his own ease and security above the most laudable of philanthropies.

To be in love is merely to be in a state of perpetual anaesthesis—to mistake an ordinary young man for a Greek god or an ordinary young woman for a goddess.

Love is the delusion that one woman differs from another.

Bachelors know more about women than married men. If they did not they would be married too.

Jarno Pennanen   (Finnish: 1881-1945)

But how then can we love?—Pick a flower together, the flower will teach you.

Not time, but its fulfillment carries meaning in love.

Juan Ramón Jiménez (Spanish: 1881-1958)

Love, you are eternal like springtime.

Pablo Picasso (Spanish: 1881-1973)

Love is the greatest refreshment in life.

P.G. Wodehouse (English: 1881-1975)

There are men who fear repartee in a wife more keenly than a sword.

James Joyce (Irish: 1882-1941)

Always see a fellow's weak point in his wife.

. . . there is nothing like a kiss long and hot down to your soul almost paralyzes you . . .

John Barrymore (American: 1882-1942)

The way to fight a woman is with your hat. Grab it and run.

Zoltán Kodály   (Hungarian: 1882-1967)

Do not say that you are an old woman! You are an eternal woman.

William Carlos Williams   (American: 1883-1963)

Love is unwordly and nothing comes of it but love.

Eleanor Roosevelt   (American: 1884-1962)

The giving of love is an education in itself.

Jerzy Leszczynski   (Polish: 1884-1977)

Quite a few married couples prove that misfortunes come in pairs.

D.H. Lawrence   (English: 1885-1930)

Death is the only pure, beautiful conclusion of a great passion.

Sex and a cocktail: they both lasted about as long, had the same effect, and amounted to about the same thing.

For while we have sex on the mind, we truly have none in the body.

When Eve ate this particular apple, she became aware of her woman-hood, mentally. And mentally she began to experiment with it. She has been experimenting ever since. So has man. To the rage and horror of both of them.

Isak Dinesen (Danish: 1885-1962)

Love, with very young people, is a heartless business. We drink at that age from thirst, or to get drunk; it is only later in life that we occupy ourselves with the individuality of our wine.

V.A. Koskenniemi (Finnish: 1885-1962)

Love's most delicate stage is experienced before either party is aware of the nature of their emotion. As soon as either one utters the word "love," its greatest spell is broken.

François Mauriac (French: 1885-1970)

To love someone is to be the only one to see a miracle invisible to others.

Love is the heart's novel, and pleasure its history.

Human love is often but the encounter of two weaknesses.

Paul Geraldy (French: 1885-1983)

It is the woman who chooses the man who will choose her.

Kersti Bergroth (Finnish: b. 1886)

Real love is always rather even and secure. The "storms" of love are selfishness.

The only real love is unhappy love. Happy love is like a healthy person's heartbeat: It goes unnoticed.

Harold Nicolson (English: 1886-1968)

The great secret of a successful marriage is to treat all disasters like incidents and none of the incidents as disasters.

Vincenzo Cardarelli (Italian: 1887-1959)

We must know that love is the flame of life and makes time worthwhile.

Swami Sivananda Sarasvati (Indian: 1887-1963)

The positive always defeats the negative: Courage overcomes fear, patience overcomes anger and irritability, Love overcomes hatred.

Hugo Dionizy Steinhaus (Polish: 1887-1972)

Love makes discoveries, dissipation makes inventions.

Alexis Léger, Saint-John Perse   (French: 1887-1975)

Love's pleasure lasts but a moment, Love's pain lasts a lifetime.

No one should die before he has loved.

Theodor Reik   (Austrian-American: b. 1888)

Work and love—these are the basics. Without them there is neurosis.

Heywood Broun   (American: 1888-1939)

The ability to make love frivolously is the chief characteristic which distinguishes human beings from beasts.

T. S. Eliot   (American: 1888-1965)

Love compels cruelty to those who do not understand love.

Love is most nearly itself when here and now cease to matter.

Giuseppe Ungaretti   (Italian: 1888-1970)

True love is a quiet, shining light.

Ivan Kurak   (Chuvash: 1889-1942)

Her life was well-spent, until the time they came to her father's house
to marry her to a foreign man.

Gabriela Mistral   (Chilean: 1889-1957)

He kissed me and now I am somebody else.

Franz Werfel   (Austrian: 1890-1945)

The basic formula for all sin is: frustrated or neglected love.

Sir A.P. Herbert   (English: 1890-1971)

The critical period in matrimony is breakfast-time.

Jean Rhys   (Dominican: 1890-1979)

Love was a terrible thing. You poisoned it and stabbed at it and
knocked it down into the mud—well down—and it got up and
staggered on, bleeding and muddy and awful. Like—like Rasputin.

Katherine Ann Porter   (American: 1890-1980)

Love must be learned, and learned again and again; there is
no end to it.

Vladislav Vancura   (Czech: 1891-1942)

Pain and love are like Geminis. This dual tree grows up from only
one root and bears both bitter and sweet fruit.

Love is a medicine for violence and a little key to the
mystery of the world.

János Bókay   (Hungarian: 1892-1961)

Only a woman can truly defend a man: a mother or a lover.

Pearl S. Buck   (American: 1892-1973)

Love dies only when growth stops.

The bitterest creature under heaven is the wife who discovers that her
husband's bravery is only bravado, that his strength is only a uniform,
that his power is but a gun in the hands of a fool.

Archibald MacLeish   (American: 1892-1982)

Love in reason's terms, answers nothing. We say that Amor vincit omnia *but in truth love conquers nothing—certainly not death— certainly not chance.*

Cole Porter   (American: 1893-1964)

Most gentlemen don't like love, they just like to kick it around.

Julian Tuwim   (Polish: 1894-1953)

Tragedy: to fall in love with a face, and marry the whole woman.

A virtuous girl never chases after boys; who ever saw a mousetrap chasing mice?

Aldous Huxley   (English: 1894-1963)

. . . love is as necessary to human beings as food and shelter; and finally the value of intelligence, without which love is impotent and freedom unattainable.

King Vidor   (American: 1895-1982)

Marriage isn't a word . . . it's a sentence!

Robert Graves (English: 1895-1985)

Love without hope, as when the young bird-catcher swept off his tall hat to the Squire's own daughter, so let the imprisoned larks escape and fly singing about her head, as she rode by.

Love may be blind, but Love at least knows what is man and what mere beast.

Giuseppe Tomasi Lampedusa (Sicilian: 1896-1957)

Love, certainly love, fires and flames for a year, then ashes for thirty years.

Frances X. Giaccone (Italian: ?1896-1977)

One with love in his breast has spurs in his side.

Love is the currency minted in God's bank.

Thornton Wilder (American: 1897-1975)

Marriage is a bribe to make a housekeeper think she's a householder.

C.S. Lewis (English: 1898-1963)

Gratitude looks to the past and love to the present.

Erno Mihályfi (Hungarian: 1898-1972)

If man is not ready for love, he can be surrounded by a thousand women, he won't even notice them. He has to be ready within . . .

Ernest Hemingway (American: 1899-1961)

When you love you wish to do things for. You wish to sacrifice for. You wish to serve.

Magdalena Samozwaniec (Polish: 1899-1972)

Friendship after love is like smoke after a fire.

Love is when someone of the opposite sex shares the good opinion we have of ourselves.

Duke Ellington (American: 1899-1974)

Love is supreme and unconditional; like is nice but limited.

Jorge Luis Borges (Argentinian: 1899-1986)

To fall in love is to create a religion that has a fallible god.

Xuan Dieu (Vietnamese: 20th century)

How is love to be explained, and what does it mean? One evening it captivates us with its gentle sunlight, its fluffy clouds, and its plaintive breeze.

Thomas Wolfe (American: 1900-1938)

There is no sight on earth more appealing than the sight of a woman making dinner for someone she loves.

Antoine de Saint-Exupéry (French: 1900-1944)

Life has taught us that love does not consist in gazing at each other but in looking outward together in the same direction.

Zora Neale Hurston (American: 1901-1960)

Love, I find is like singing. Everybody can do enough to satisfy themselves, though it may not impress the neighbors as being very much.

André Malraux (French: 1901-1976)

Love, what is it? A cork and a bottle.

Marcel Petiet   (French: b. 1902)

> *Love is the yearning for the unknown carried into madness.*

Langston Hughes   (American: 1902-1967)

> *When peoples care for you and cry for you, they can straighten out your soul.*

Countee Cullen   (American: 1903-1946)

> *The loss of love is a terrible thing; they lie who say that death is worse.*
>
> *Never love with all your heart, it only ends in aching.*

Xavier Villaurrutia   (Mexican: 1903-1950)

> *My love is like the dark honeycomb of deep red shadow which the hermetic pomegranate produces within its concave walls.*

Anaïs Nin   (French-American: 1903-1977)

> *The language of sex is yet to be invented. The language of the senses is yet to be explored.*

Tito Colliander   (Finnish: b. 1904)

Instinct seeks satisfaction. Love is free of all demands.

Michal Choromanksi   (Polish: 1904-1972)

A woman surrenders herself only to someone she does not love.

Pablo Neruda   (Chilean: 1904-1973)

Love is so short, forgetting is so long.

Simone Beck   (French: 1904-1991)

*Making love without love is like trying to make a soufflé
without egg whites.*

Jean-Paul Sartre   (French: 1905-1980)

*When we love animals and children too much, we love them at the ex-
pense of men.*

Samuel Beckett   (Irish: 1906-1989)

The desert of loneliness and recrimination that men call love.

W.H. Auden   (American: 1907-1973)

Among those whom I like or admire, I can find no common denomi-
nator, but among those whom I love, I can: all of them
make me laugh.

Boleslaw Szczesny Herbaczewski   (Polish: b. 1908)

The most terrible thing for a woman is unfulfilled desire. The most
terrible thing for a man is fulfilled desire.

Cesare Pavese   (Italian: 1908-1950)

No woman marries for money: they are all clever enough, before
marrying a millionaire, to fall in love with him first.

Theodore Roethke   (American: 1908-1963)

Love begets love. This torment is my joy.

Jan Noha   (Czech: 1908-1966)

With love it's better to live even the simple, ordinary day.

Bohdan Ihor Antonych   (Ukrainian: 1909-1937)

Only those who kiss for the first time, know how to kiss with passion.

Stanislaw Jerzy Lec   (Polish: 1909-1966)

Hay smells different to lovers and horses.

Árpád Berczik   (Hungarian: b. 1910)

First examine the mother, then marry the daughter.

Jean Anouilh   (French: 1910-1987)

Love is, above all, the gift of oneself.

Gian Carol Menotti   (American: b. 1911)

Love is born of faith, lives on hope, and dies of charity.

Eugène Ionesco   (Romanian-French: 1912-1994)

*It is our own mediocrity that makes us let go of love, makes us re-
nounce it. True love doesn't know the meaning of renunciation.*

Robertson Davies (Canadian: b. 1913)

Short love is sweetest, and most love curdles if you keep it.

A. J. Seymour (Guyanese: b. 1914)

But as the unhurried stars wheel overhead above a thousand million nests of love, one or two women lie and think and glow.

Lajos Mesterházi (Hungarian: 1916-1986)

Love is our most holy and important emotion, which ties us to one another, which links us to the world, to the future; love is life's greatest joy, our only salvation from death.

Kálmán Mikszáth (Hungarian: 1916-1986)

Observe the women in a family—and you will learn what the family is like. Study the women of a country, and you will know what the nation is like.

Andree Chedid (Egyptian: b. 1920)

Others, like myself, must have felt their lives crumble away in the course of an existence devoid of love. If I cry, I cry a little for them.

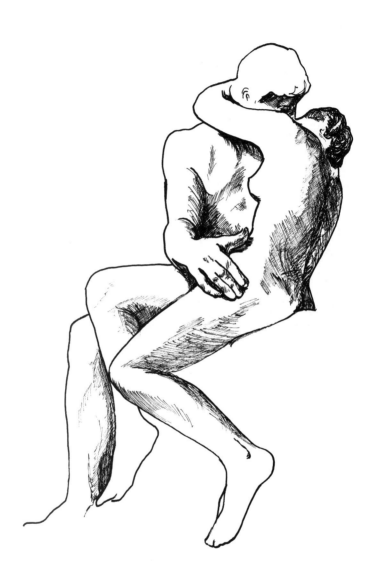

Vaclav Kubin   (Czech: b. 1920)

A kiss is an aperitif of love.

Peter Ustinov   (English: b. 1921)

*Love is an act of endless forgiveness, a tender look which
becomes a habit.*

Gyula Fekete   (Hungarian: b. 1922)

*Every biologist can tell you what love is. Only the biologist who is in
love does not know.*

Chairil Anwar   (Indonesian: 1922-1949)

Love's a danger that quickly fades.

Norman Mailer   (American: b. 1923)

*Love is simple to understand if you haven't got a mind soft and full of
holes. It's a crutch, that's all, and there isn't one of us that doesn't
need a crutch.*

Love is dialectic, man, back and forth, hate and sweet.

Endre Nagy (Hungarian: b. 1923)

Marriage is a workshop, wherein two people with wisdom, patience and mutual self-denial, work towards their happiness. It is like the fertile field: it gives back bounteously that which is sown.

. . . why do they say that love is all powerful? Because, it can create the miracle of making two people bearable to one another.

True love is a program for life, because it represents a life-long task.

Yehuda Amichai (Israeli: b. 1924)

Love is like a reservoir of kindness and pleasure, like silos and pools during a siege.

Yoshiyuki Junnosake (Japanese: b. 1924)

To be in love with someone . . . is to appropriate as part of one's own self—which means that one's self-regard is doubled.

Barouyr Sevag (Armenian: 1924-1972)

Your unripe love and my too ripe want, like the edges of the legendary sword of chastity, keep us two cool blades apart.

James Baldwin   (American: 1924-1987)

The face of love is an unknown, precisely because it is invested with so much of oneself. It is a mystery, containing, like all mysteries, the possibility of torment.

Vasyl' Ivanchuk   (Ukrainian: b. 1927)

Love—a bit of a headache, a dose of heartache.

Iain Chrichton Smith   (Scottish: b. 1928)

Love is incessant climbing to far peaks, ambitious haunting.

Eeva Kilpi   (Finnish: b. 1928)

I cannot manage friendship: It requires too much. I know how to love. It requires only one participant.

Naukatjik   (Eskimo: quoted in 1929)

Women become dangerous when they have no husbands to lie with them.

Milan Kundera (Czech: b. 1929)

Love does not make itself felt in the desire for copulation (a desire that extends to an infinite number of women) but in the desire for shared sleep (a desire limited to one woman).

Ursula Le Guin (American: b. 1929)

Love doesn't just sit there, like a stone, it has to be made, like bread, remade all the time, made new.

Lorraine Hansberry (American: 1930-1965)

There is always something left to love. And if you ain't learned that, you ain't learned nothing.

Desmond Tutu (South African: b. 1931)

When a chap is in love, he will go out in all kinds of weather to keep an appointment with his beloved. Love can be demanding, in fact more demanding than law. It has its own imperatives—think of a mother sitting by the bedside of a sick child through the night, impelled only by love. Nothing is too much trouble for love.

Sylvia Plath   (American: 1932-1963)

Love is a shadow—how can you lie and cry after it?

V.S. Naipaul   (West Indian: b. 1932)

But machismo is about the conquest and humiliation of women.

Calvin Trillin   (American: b. 1935)

Marriage, as I have often remarked, is not merely sharing one's fettucine but sharing the burden of finding the fettucine restaurant in the first place.

George Davis   (American: b. 1939)

In love you find the oddest combinations: Materialistic people find themselves in love with idealists. Clingers fall in love with players; … homebodies capture and try to smother butterflies. If it weren't so serious we could laugh at it.

Petr Skarland   (Czech: b. 1939)

Love is like a work in dreams. To be in love and alone, it means to find words that were lost a long time ago.

Matti J. Kuronen   (Finnish: b. 1940)

Closeness without conflict exists only in the cemetery.

Thaweesuk Thongthawan   (Thai: b. 1941)

The heart that blindly rushes to love, if broken, where lies its dignity?

Billy Connolly   (American: b. 1942)

Marriage is a wonderful invention; but, then again, so is a bicycle repair kit.

Nikki Giovanni   (American: b. 1943)

And love is only and always about the lover and never the beloved.

Helena Vajgantova   (Czech: b. 1948)

[Love] is like a snake that soothes before it kills with its poison.

Bilingual Love Poetry from Hippocrene

Treasury of African Love Poems & Proverbs

Treasury of Arabic Love Poems, Quotations & Proverbs

Treasury of Czech Love Poems, Quotations & Proverbs

Treasury of Finnish Love Poems, Quotations & Proverbs

*Treasury of French Love Poems, Quotations & Proverbs**

*Treasury of German Love Poems, Quotations & Proverbs**

*Treasury of Hungarian Love Poems, Quotations & Proverbs**

*Treasury of Italian Love Poems, Quotations & Proverbs**

*Treasury of Jewish Love Poems, Quotations & Proverbs**

*Treasury of Polish Love Poems, Quotations & Proverbs**

Treasury of Roman Love Poems, Quotations & Proverbs

*Treasury of Russian Love Poems, Quotations & Proverbs**

*Treasury of Spanish Love Poems Quotations & Proverbs**

*Treasury of Ukrainian Love Poems, Quotations & Proverbs**

* Also available as an Audio Book

HIPPOCRENE BOOKS, INC.
171 Madison Avenue
New York, NY 10016

Bilingual Love Stories from Hippocrene . . .

Treasury of Classic French Love Short Stories
in French and English
edited by Lisa Neal
This beautiful gift volume includes six classic French love stories from Marie de France, Marguerite de Navarre, Madame de Lafayette, and Guy de Maupassant and others.
159 pages • 5 x 7
0-7818-0511-2 • $11.95hc • (621)

Treasury of Classic Spanish Love Short Stories
in Spanish and English
edited by Bonnie May
A lovely gift volume including five classic tales of love from Cervantes, Miguel de Unamuno, Jorge de Montemayor and Gustavo Adolfo Becquer among others.
157 pages • 5 x 7
0-7818-0512-0 • $11.95hc • (604)

Treasury of Classic Polish Love Short Stories
in Polish and English
edited by Miroslaw Lipinski
This volume delves into Poland's rich literary tradition to bring you classic love stories from five renowned authors. It explores love's many romantic, joyous, as well as melancholic facets.
109 pages • 5 x 7
0-7818-0513-9 • $11.95hc • (603)

Treasury of Classic Russian Love Short Stories
in Russian and English
by Anton Chekov
This beautiful new addition to the love stories series inlcudes three classic tales of love: "The Kiss," "Lady with a Lapdog," and "On Love," from Anton Chekov, noted nineteenth century Russian playwright and short story writer. The original Russian text is displayed side by side with its English translation.
128 pages • 5 x 7
0-7818-0601-1 • $11.95hc • (674)

Also available from Hippocrene . . .

Classic English Love Poems
edited by Emile Capouya
A charmingly illustrated gift edition which includes 95 classic poems of love from English writers.
130 pages • 6 x 9 • $17.50hc
0-7818-0572-4 • (671)

Classic French Love Poems
This volume contains over 25 beautiful illustrations by famous artist Maurice Leloir and 120 inspiring poems translated into English from French, the language of love itself.
130 pages • 6 x 9 • $17.50hc
0-7818-0573-2 • (672)

Hebrew Love Poems
edited by David C. Gross
Includes 90 love lyrics from biblical times to modern day, with illustrations by Shagra Weil.
91 pages • 6 x 9 • $14.95pb
0-7818-0430-2 • (473)

Irish Love Poems: Dánta Grá
edited by Paula Redes
This striking collection includes illustrations by Peadar McDaid and poems that span four centuries up to the most modern of poets, Nuala Ni Dhomhnaill, Brendan Kennelly, and Nobel prize winner, Seamus Heaney.
146 pages • 6 x 9 • $17.50hc
0-7818-0396-9 • (70)

Scottish Love Poems: A Personal Anthology
edited by Lady Antonia Fraser
Lady Fraser collects the loves and passions of her fellow Scots, from Burns to Aileen Campbell Nye, into a book that will find a way to touch everyone's heart.
253 pages • 5 ½ x 8 ¼ • $14.95pb
0-7818-0406-X • (482)

Treasury of Love Proverbs from Many Lands
compiled by the editors at Hippocrene and illustrated by Rosemary Fox

Love and let everyone know; hate and be silent.
  —*Egypt*

He who waits for his lover hears the footsteps of the spirits.
  —*Nigeria*

A life without love is like a year without summer.
  —*Sweden*

This groundbreaking multicultural anthology includes over 600 proverbs on love from over 50 lands and languages. These proverbs address such timeless experiences as first love, the pain of love, jealousy, marriage, the heart, attraction and flirtation, and unrequited love. A beautiful gift volume with charming illustrations throughout.

146 pages • 6 x 9 • illustrations • $17.50hc
0-7818-0563-5 • (698)

All prices subject to change. **TO PURCHASE HIPPOCRENE BOOKS** contact your local bookstore, call (718) 454-2366, or write to: HIPPOCRENE BOOKS, 171 Madison Avenue, New York, NY 10016. Please enclose check or money order, adding $5.00 shipping (UPS) for the first book and $.50 for each additional book.